*P*ray *for O*ur *N*ation

Harrison House
Tulsa, Oklahoma

Unless otherwise indicated, all Scripture
quotations are taken from the *King James
Version of the Bible.*

Direct quotations from the Bible appear in bold type.

05 04 03 02 01   10 09 08 07 06 05

Pray for Our Nation
ISBN 1-57794-254-X
Copyright © 1999 by Harrison House
P.O. Box 35035
Tulsa, OK 74153

Published by Harrison House, Inc.
P.O. Box 35035
Tulsa, OK 74153

Contents

Part 4—Prayers for the Spiritual Growth of Our Nation

Introduction

Faith, courage, and prayer birthed our great nation and guided America through more than 200 years of wars, natural disasters and national crisis.

Prayer is a freedom guaranteed to us by our Constitution, and a God-given right to all humanity. The opportunity to pray is a privilege, honor and sacred duty.

History has proven that forces will wage war against our freedom. Terrorism has shed blood on American soil. Violent crime has invaded American homes and schools. Drugs and alcohol abuse rage against the innocence of our youth. Forces of darkness threaten our morality, integrity and faith. Prayer for our nation is our defense.

Now is the time to be resolute in our defiance against the forces of destruction— to unite as a nation and not succumb to fear. Americans must stand strong and remain bold in faith, courage and prayers.

The nation needs your prayers. The president, his advisors, Congress and all local and national leaders need your prayers. The armed forces, firefighters and law enforcement personnel need your prayers.

Often people are unsure how to pray. This book is designed to provide answers to your questions. It is the sincerity of the heart that determines a successful prayer, not the length, eloquence or level of vocabulary. Each prayer is based on biblical Scriptures so that you can pray in confidence, knowing you are praying God's will for this nation. The table of contents is listed by topic allowing your prayers to be directed according to your individual needs and concerns.

Make a commitment to pray daily for your nation. Pray the prayers included within these pages with heart, purpose and passion. Minutes can change crisis into hope when you take the time to pray. Your heavenly Father is listening. He loves you and this nation.

The Publisher

If my people, which are called by my name, shall humble themselves, and pray, and seek my face, and turn from their wicked ways; then will I hear from heaven, and will forgive their sin, and will heal their land.

—2 Chronicles 7:14

PART 1

Prayers for the Leaders of Our Nation

1
The President

Dear Father, in Jesus' name I lift up our president to You. I know that our leader's heart is in Your hand, so I ask You to guide the head of our nation in the way You would have him to go.

Father, I pray that You would surround our president with wise counsel—men and women of integrity who place Your agenda and the good of this nation above their own and whose motives are for that which is right.

I pray that You would give our leader discernment, understanding and knowledge so that our nation may know stability internally and abroad.

I give thanks for our president according to Your Word and thank You for working in and through his leadership so that we might lead peaceable lives in godliness and honesty.

Scripture References

1 Timothy 2:1,2
Romans 13:1 NAS
Proverbs 28:2 AMP
Proverbs 21:1 NAS
Proverbs 16:10 AMP
Proverbs 8:15 NIV

Direct my thought, words and work, wash away my sins in the immaculate Blood of the Lamb, and purge my heart by Thy Holy Spirit.... Daily frame me more and more into the likeness of Thy Son Jesus Christ.

—GEORGE WASHINGTON,
1ST U.S. PRESIDENT

2
The Congress

Dear Father, I come to You in the mighty name of Jesus, thanking You and praising You for our great nation. I thank You for the plan You gave to our forefathers by which to govern our nation and for the division of powers so that our destiny does not rest in the hands of one person.

In praying for those in authority, I therefore lift up our Congress (both the House of Representatives and the Senate). I pray that, by Your power, our legislative body would make laws that are just.

Father, I ask You to give them wisdom to make decisions that would strengthen and prosper our nation. I desire that they would make right decisions concerning the politics, the social welfare and the economics of our nation.

I pray that You would cause Congress to be motivated more by Your hand than by partisan or personal concerns.

———

Scripture References

Proverbs 8:15 NIV
Proverbs 19:21
Proverbs 29:14
Proverbs 21:30
Proverbs 15:22

———

Remember that God is our only sure trust.

—MARY WASHINGTON,
GEORGE WASHINGTON'S MOTHER

3
Decisions in National Crisis

Father God, in the name of Jesus I pray that You would direct the leaders of this nation in times of crisis. Grant them wisdom and understanding, and help them to respond quickly and effectively to each situation. May divinely directed decisions be on their lips, and may they do that which is right in Your sight. May they follow Your will to direct our nation in the paths of peace and safety.

Unite all response agencies in an organized and harmonious fashion to bring quick and effective resolve to the demands of this crisis.

Empower us as United States citizens to do our part, financially, physically, emotionally and spiritually to support all who have been affected by this tragedy.

I pray that You encourage and strengthen our Nation. Surround us with Your love and mercy. Bring peace and comfort to all those who are suffering as a result of this crisis.

———

Scripture Reference

Proverbs 16:10 AMP
Proverbs 11:3-6

———

Renewing our knowledge of and faith in God through Holy Scripture can strengthen us as a nation and a people.

—THE YEAR OF THE BIBLE
WAS DECLARED IN 1983 BY
A JOINT RESOLUTION OF
THE HOUSE AND SENATE

4
The Economy

Dear Father, in the name of the Lord Jesus, I pray for our nation's economy. I know that even more than a strong military, a strong economy helps keep a nation powerful.

Father, I pray that You would raise up people of skill and wisdom who will affect the economy of our nation. Give them inspired ideas and a voice with the powers that be.

Cause Congress to vote aright in these matters. Give them foresight so that provision might be made for our nation's future, not just its present.

Father, as the people of our nation continue to finance the preaching of the gospel and help the poor all over the world, I pray that You would continue to prosper us more and more.

Scripture Reference

Matthew 18:18-20
Deuteronomy 8:17,18
Deuteronomy 28:12
Psalm 112:1-3

While we give praise to God, the supreme disposer of all events, for His interposition on our behalf, let us guard against the dangerous error of trusting in, or boasting of, an arm of flesh....

If your case is just, if your principles are pure, and if your conduct is prudent, you need not fear the multitude of opposing hosts.

—JOHN WITHERSPOON,
A SIGNER OF THE DECLARATION
OF INDEPENDENCE

5
Supreme Court Justices

Father, in the name of Jesus, I bring our
Supreme Court justices before You.
Knowing that they are appointed of man, I
pray that You would influence the selection
of each new replacement. May they be
people who will judge rightly in every matter
brought before them.

As our Supreme Court makes its decisions,
I pray that its decrees would be Your
decrees. I desire that, by Your hand, godly
justice would rise up within our justices and
that they would make rulings in line with
Your will.

I pray that they would set a standard of
justice and balance for the judicial office at

large, not only on a national level but for every adjudicator in our nation.

We give You thanks, dear Father, knowing it is Your good pleasure and will to work in every level of government.

———

Scripture References

Proverbs 8:14-16
Deuteronomy 16:18
2 Samuel 23:3
Proverbs 11:1

———

*There are a good many problems
before the American people today,
and before me as President, but I expect
to find the solution to those problems
just in the proportion that I am faithful
in the study of the Word of God.*

—WOODROW WILSON,
28TH U.S. PRESIDENT

6
Law Enforcement Officers

Dear Father, I thank You that we live in a nation governed by the rule of law. For that reason I pray for all persons involved in the law enforcement in our nation.

In the name of Jesus, I pray that You will prosper their endeavors. Give them wisdom in crime prevention as well as prosecution. Bring persons of integrity and dedication to the force. Grace them to do their jobs efficiently and effectively.

Give them supernatural insight and wisdom in the location and capture of desperate criminals. Grant them divine intervention in finding kidnapped and lost persons. Help them in their searches and rescues, so that more people will be recovered safe and alive.

And, Father, I pray for the protection of our law enforcement officers at home and abroad. May they escape death and injury and bring others to safety as well.

Scripture Reference

Romans 13:1-5 NIV

Remember ever; and always, that your country was founded...by the stern old Puritans who made the deck of the Mayflower an altar of the living God, and whose first act on touching the soil of the new world was to offer on bended knees thanksgiving to Almighty God.

—HENRY WILSON,
18TH U.S. VICE PRESIDENT
UNDER ULYSSES S. GRANT

Pray for Our Nation

7
Election of Godly Leaders

Father, I desire to vote intelligently in all elections. I pray that You will bring to light the things I need to know so I may vote in line with Your plan, will and purpose.

May things not only come to light for the Christian community, but may things be made clear to the unbelieving community as well. I pray that what is right would be so clear that even unbelievers would vote using wisdom and demanding honesty and uprightness from their politicians.

Dear Father, in the name of Jesus, may the citizens of our nation become so weary of sin and degradation in our nation's leaders that they will begin to seek out godly leaders to represent them on every level of government. Give such leaders favor with the public and the media.

Father, make our nation a fragrance in the earth, a force to be reckoned with, a hand extended to those in need.

Scripture References

Luke 12:1-3
John 16:13

If we work on marble, it will perish; if on brass, time will efface it; if we rear up temples, they will crumble into dust; but if we work upon immortal minds and imbue them with principles, with the just fear of God and the love of our fellow men, we engrave on those tablets something that will brighten to all eternity.

—DANIEL WEBSTER,
AMERICAN POLITICIAN

8
Prayer for Christians To Vote

Dear Father, I do not take lightly what You have done in our nation. I appreciate not only the right but the privilege I have to vote. I pray that I, as well as others, will use that privilege wisely, seeking Your will as we consider the qualifications of those for whom we are to vote.

I pray for my Christian family (the body of Christ) that they would see the right to vote as a gift from Your hand and avail themselves of this opportunity.

May there arise such a force of righteousness in our electoral system that it would affect every realm and level of government in our nation.

I pray in Jesus' name that the powers that be would gain a profound respect not only for the political strength of the Christian community but for our spiritual influence in our nation as well.

Scripture References

Luke 6:13

Acts 6:1-6

Oh, Lord, Thou hast told us how to pray. Help us to shut the door, shutting out the world, and the enemy and any fear or doubt which spoils prayer. May there be no distance between our souls and Thee.

—JOHN WANAMAKER,
AMERICAN MERCHANT AND U.S.
POSTMASTER GENERAL FROM 1889-93

9
Foreign Relations

Father, in the name of Jesus, I pray for the international relations of my nation. I pray that You would cause us to have favor in the nations of the earth.

I pray that because of our international influence, doors would open in nations that have been closed to the gospel in the past. I pray those You raise up would give favor to the missionaries in their respective nations.

Raise up wise men and women to fill our diplomatic corps, persons of skill and understanding in foreign affairs and in the affairs of state.

Grant favor to our embassy personnel on every foreign front, so they will be able to maintain good relations in their respective posts and so that even our enemies will be at peace with them.

Scripture References

Proverbs 16:7
Mark 16:15
Matthew 28:18,19

God would graciously pour out His Holy Spirit on us to bring us to a thorough Repentance and effectual Reformation that our iniquities may not be our ruin; that He would restore, preserve and secure the Liberties of this and all the other British American colonies, and make the Land a mountain of Holiness, and Habitation of Righteousness forever.

—JONATHAN TRUMBALL,
AMERICAN POET

10
Safety of Diplomats

Father, in the name of Jesus, I pray that
You would exalt our nation to such a degree
that even the most fanatical of our enemies
would fear attacking our embassies and
their personnel.

Rather, Lord, let our enemies begin to see
our nation as an ensign of peace to the
world and realize that living in peace is
prefereable to living in fear and bondage.

Supernaturally alert our personnel of any
potential attacks, and give them the power
to quell them before they happen.

Father, I ask You to send laborers for the
Lord to embassy personnel worldwide so

they may hear the gospel and find the divine protection You provide for believers.

———

Scripture References

Proverbs 16:7
Matthew 28:18,19
Mark 16:15

———

We all can pray. We all should pray.
We should ask the fulfillment of God's will.
We should ask for courage, wisdom,
for the quietness of soul which comes alone
to them who place their lives in His hands.

—HARRY S. TRUMAN,
33RD U.S. PRESIDENT

PART 2

Prayers for the Social Welfare of Our Nation

11
National Morality

Father, I know that the spirit of the world creeps into the body of Christ almost unawares sometimes, and before we know it, we can so easily be led astray and caught up in worldly actions (at times so subtly we don't even recognize what has happened to us).

So in the name of Jesus, I pray that You would raise up a voice in our nation that would rally the body of Christ and cause us to become the standard bearers to such a degree that we would profoundly affect the morality of our nation.

*Never forget, Americans, that yours is
a spiritual country. Yes, I know you're a
practical people. Like others, I've marvelled
at your factories, your skyscrapers, and your
arsenals. But underlying everything else is
the fact that America began as a God-loving,
God-fearing, God-worshipping people.*

—GENERAL ROMULO,
GENERAL OF THE PHILIPPINES

12
Schools

Father, in the name of Jesus, I pray that You would ignite our schools with holy fire, that You would continue to embolden our Christian youth to take a stand with their peers and show them the way—Jesus Christ. May they boldly speak the Word so that You may stretch forth Your hand to heal and do signs and wonders in the name of Jesus Christ.

May there be such a move of Your grace and power in our nation's school systems that alcohol, drugs, guns, pornography and illicit sexual activity cease to be issues.

May the fear of the Lord prevail in our schools to the degree that no one would dare to transgress.

———

Scripture References

2 Chronicles 34:1,2
Acts 4:29,30
Acts 5:12-14
Psalm 71:17

———

America was founded by people who believe[d] that God was their rock of safety. I recognize we must be cautious in claiming that God is on our side, but I think it's all right to keep asking if we're on His side.

—RONALD REAGAN,
40TH U.S. PRESIDENT

13
The Educational System

Dear Father, in the name of Jesus, I pray for all those who are in authority in our national educational system. I pray that the decisions they make would be by Your guidance.

Please help those in authority see that "separation of church and state" does not mean godless education.

May there be such a revival in our nation that those in power must acquiesce in that which is right in Your sight.

May our goal be not only to understand the students, but to bring them to understanding both on a moral and intellectual level.

Cause our educational system to be preeminent in the world. And may discipline and respect be restored to our nation's schools.

———

Scripture References

1 Timothy 2:1,2
Deuteronomy 4:5,6
Proverbs 1:2-5

———

The time has come to turn to God and reassert our trust in Him for the healing of America.... Our country is in need of and ready for a spiritual renewal.

—RONALD REAGAN,
40TH U.S. PRESIDENT

14
Educators

Father, in the name of Jesus, I pray that You would raise up godly educators who are dedicated to their field and can capture the hearts and minds of our nation's youth on each level of education.

I sincerely ask that our educators will pray unceasingly for guidance and wisdom to become the examples to their students that You would wish them to be and that the students would be receptive to that dedication on the part of their teachers.

May the standard of excellence be restored in our institutions of learning so that our educators would be prepared to pass on the spirit of excellence.

May they be empowered to require
excellence and reprove sloth and ignorance.

———

Scripture References

1 Peter 2:21
Ecclesiastes 7:12
Ecclesiastes 2:13

———

*I thank God that I live in a country
where dreams can come true, where failure
sometimes is the first step to success and
where success is only another form of failure
if we forget what our priorities should be.*

—HARRY LLOYD HOPKINS,
ADVISOR TO FRANKLIN D. ROOSEVELT

15
Racial Harmony

Dear Father, I realize that racial enmity came as a result of the Fall. Truly, we do not even know what ethnicity Adam was, except that he was Your creation and it is from his seed that all humanity proceeded.

I pray in Jesus' name that there would be such a move of Your Spirit in our nation, that our oneness in Christ Jesus would positively influence relations between races.

I desire that this first begin in the body of Christ and spread throughout every community in our country.

May it affect every ethnic group in our nation and cross every racial barrier.

I pray that when we look at those from another culture, we won't see them as people of another color but that we will see them through eyes of love as You see them—as people created in your image.

———

Scripture References

Galatians 3:27, 28
Revelation 5:9

———

Prayer is the contemplation of the facts of life from the highest point of view.

—RALPH WALDO EMERSON,
AMERICAN AUTHOR

16
National Patriotism

Father, I pray in Jesus' name that You would restore a social conscience to our nation.

I pray that we would again see the value of teaching our children the virtue of being good citizens—to not only live for the good of the individual but the good of others as well.

Dear Father, I desire to see our nation restored to godly integrity and excellence, so that our children and our citizens can be proud of their nation and proud to be called citizens of it.

In recognizing our duty to God and our country, keep us mindful to pray for our nation not only in our churches and our homes, but also in the quietness of our daily lives.

*Prayer covers the whole of man's life.
There is no thought, feeling, yearning, or
desire, however low, trifling, or vulgar
we may deem it, which, if it affects our
real interest or happiness, we may not
lay before God.... The whole burden of
the whole life of every man may be
rolled on to God and not weary him,
though it has wearied the man.*

—HENRY WARD BEECHER,
AMERICAN CLERGYMAN

41

17
The Media

Dear Father, in Jesus' name, may there be such a revival in our nation that it will affect every area of the media.

May the church be so revived and may there be such an gathering of believers that they neither will tolerate media "hype" nor support whatever would fuel it.

May the media find it profitable and ethical to publish the truth and broadcast the effects of Your mighty hand in our nation.

I desire that You would raise up journalists and publishers of integrity, who would speak, write and print the truth in the face of all opposition.

Father, send laborers to speak to those in media circles, that they may come to the saving knowledge of Jesus Christ.

———

Scripture References

Proverbs 14:34
Psalm 68:11

———

The only limit to our realization of tomorrow will be our doubts of today. Let us move forward with strong and active faith.

—FRANKLIN D. ROOSEVELT,
32ND U.S. PRESIDENT

PART 3

Prayers for the Safety of Our Nation

18
Protection for the Body of Christ

Dear Father, I thank You that we are not appointed to wrath and that we have nothing to fear, because You are with us. I lift up the issue of terrorism, both at home and abroad, and I pray in Jesus' name that Your great ability to save, protect and deliver would come to light in the body of Christ and in the world.

Father, I remember the great deliverance You afforded Moses and the children of Israel so they could escape from the Egyptians unharmed. I know that because You did that for the seed of Abraham under an older and lesser covenant, You will certainly do that and more for Your children under this new and better covenant.

I choose life and deliverance in the name of Jesus Christ. I thank You for the angels who have charge over my life, who protect me and keep me in all my endeavors.

Scripture References

Exodus 14:10-30
2 Kings 6:15-17
1 Thessalonians 5:9
1 John 4:4
Psalm 91:11,12
Hebrews 1:13,14
Exodus 11:7
Matthew 18:18-20

The men who have guided the destiny of the United States have found the strength for their tasks by going to their knees.

—LYNDON B. JOHNSON,
36TH U.S. PRESIDENT

19
National Protection

Most High God, I come to You in the name of Jesus, asking for divine protection for the people of this nation. I pray for the safety of every man, woman and child. Keep us from harms way and provide protection from plans of destruction that our enemies have plotted. Stop strategies of destruction that our enemies would try to evoke.

Give wisdom, understanding and discernment to those who provide protection. Help us to be watchful and alert to signs of wrongdoing.

Provide insight to national and local authorities on ways to guard, defend and insure the safety of all American citizens both at home and abroad. Help us to unite with government leaders and law enforcement personnel in making this country a safe place to live, work and play; allowing Americans to enjoy freedom without fear.

Scripture References

John 16:13
Romans 8:14
Matthew 18:19, 20

Our prayer and God's mercy are like two buckets in a well; while the one ascends the other descends.

—MARY HOPKINS,
U.S. EDUCATOR

20
Protection From Nuclear and Chemical Weapons

Father, I thank You that You make a difference between the righteous and the unrighteous. If You spared Israel from the Egyptians, You will spare Your people now. As You would have spared Sodom and Gomorrah for the sake of ten righteous people, so, too, I pray will You spare the cities of our nation for the sake of the righteous.

Therefore, I pray in the name of the Lord Jesus that You will alert us of any hidden dangers, that we might pray as the need arises.

I pray You would keep our nation strong, so that our might would deter offenders.

Satan, in the name of the Lord Jesus Christ, I bind you and forbid any weapon to operate against our nation.

Scripture References

Isaiah 54:14-17

2 Thessalonians 2:6,7 NIV

Genesis 18:20-33; 19:1-25

Matthew 5:13

2 Corinthians 5:21

Grudge no expense—yield to no opposition—forget fatigue—till, by the strength of prayer and sacrifice, the spirit of love shall have overcome...

—MARIA WESTON CHAPMAN,
U.S. ABOLITIONIST, EDITOR

21
Peace

Dear Father, I clearly see that it is Your will for us to dwell in peace and safety. In obedience to your Word I continue to pray, in the name of the Lord Jesus, that those in authority will make decisions to keep our nation safe, just as I pray for peace in other nations.

I pray our nation would be a blessing to Israel, that we might continue to be blessed.

I pray that the righteousness of our nation would continue to finance the preaching of the Gospel in all the world. I pray that our sending and our giving would increase.

May our nation continue to help nations that are in trouble and are less fortunate than we are.

I ask You to make our nation a blessing to all the nations of the earth.

Scripture References

1 Timothy 2:1,2

Genesis 18:23

Malachi 3:10-12

Proverbs 29:14

Isaiah 43:26

Luke 4:18,19

Genesis 18:20,21

Matthew 25:31-40

Give to us clear vision that we may know where to stand and what to stand for—because unless we stand for something, we shall fall for anything.

—PETER MARSHALL,
U.S. RELIGIOUS LEADER

22
The Military

Thank You Lord, for the men and women of our armed forces. Protect them as they protect us. Defend them as they defend us. Encourage and strengthen their spirit, soul and body in the execution of their duties and responsibilities. May they be mentally and physically strong when required to face the challenges of combat. Undergird them with Your spirit and might when they are called upon to endure the hardships of battle.

I pray that nothing would take them by surprise but that they would be aware of all potential aggression. Enable them to curtail hostile actions before they start.

Reveal to military leaders the strategies and plots that enemies would wage. Give leaders wisdom and insight in all decisions. May response to any aggression by enemies of this nation be swift, accurate and effective.

Father, give our military favor with the governmental agencies of this country. I pray that our Congress would appropriate sufficient funds to keep our nation's military preeminent in the world.

Thank You Lord, for providing America with the best trained, equipped and lead military force in the world today. Fill them with Your saving grace and the gospel of peace that they may be shining witnesses of Your love, in the name of Jesus.

Scripture References

Matthew 9:37,38
Romans 10:13-15
Psalm 119:114,117
Isaiah 41:12,13

Religious faith has the miraculous power to lift ordinary human beings to greatness in seasons of stress.

—SAM J. ERVIN, JR.,
NBA PLAYER FOR THE
SEATTLE SUPERSONICS

23
The Families of Our Military

Father, in the name of the Lord Jesus, I also lift up to You in prayer the families of our military. I pray that the gospel will extend to them, that they might know Him and the power of His resurrection.

Father, I desire that these families might be a prayer force for our nation and our military.

May they know abundance and no lack. May they be well provided for and well taken care of.

Father, give them the courage of warriors. May the peace that passes understanding sustain them in seasons of separation.

Comfort them with Your Word, that they might have faith to see their sons, daughters, husbands and wives returned to them in wholeness and safety.

Scripture References

Matthew 9:37,38
Philippians 4:7
Philippians 3:10
2 Corinthians 1:3,4

With a good conscience our only sure reward, with history the final judge of our deeds, let us go forth to lead the land we love, asking His blessing and His help, but knowing that here on God's work must truly be our own.

—JOHN F. KENNEDY,
35TH U.S. PRESIDENT

24
Veterans

Father, in the name of Jesus, I thank You for our veterans. I thank You for their willingness to risk all so that our nation might dwell in peace and safety.

May they find the honor and recognition they deserve.

In the name of Your divine Son, I pray that You will heal the physical and psychological wounds some of these veterans have suffered. Bring peace to those who mourn the loss of comrades.

Father, I pray that our nation would learn to respect and acknowledge those who have served their country well.

Scripture Reference

Romans 13:7
John 14:27
John 16:33

I pray Heaven bestow the best of blessings on this House and all that shall hereafter inhabit it. May none but honest and wise men ever rule under this roof.

—JOHN ADAMS,
2ND U.S. PRESIDENT

25
POWs

Father, in the name of Jesus, I pray for those who have been taken captive in war. Give them the courage to persevere and also the knowledge that they have not been forgotten.

May our nation find ways to rescue them safely and quickly. Guide our political negotiators in their resolute efforts to gain the freedom of these courageous people.

I pray that they will not be used as pawns to the advantage of our enemies.

When their freedom is restored, let our POWs walk with pride and dignity because of the suffering they have endured, as our grateful nation owes them a debt of honor.

Scripture References

2 Timothy 2:3
Psalm 142:7
Psalm 30:1-5

I conceive we cannot better express ourselves than by humbly supplicating the Supreme Ruler of the world...that the confusions that are and have been among the nations may be overruled by the promoting and speedily bringing in the holy and happy period when the kingdoms of our Lord and Saviour Jesus Christ may be everywhere established.

—SAMUEL ADAMS,
AMERICAN REVOLUTIONIST
AND A SIGNER OF THE
DECLARATION OF INDEPENDENCE

26
MIAs

Father, in the name of Jesus, may we find more efficient ways of tracing and identifying those who are missing in action.

Let them not be forgotten, fill them with the hope of freedom and the knowledge that their loved ones and comrades anxiously await their return.

I pray the truth would come to light quickly so that the living may be rescued and the families of the deceased may find timely closure.

For those whom You have received into eternity, we pray that the peaceful shadows of the setting sun will rest gently upon their graves.

Scripture References

Deuteronomy 29:29
John 3:21
John 8:36
1 Corinthians 15:51-55

The Lord our God be with us, as He was with our fathers; may He not leave us or forsake us; so that He may incline our hearts to Him, to walk in all His ways... that all peoples of the earth may know that the Lord is God; there is no other.

—GEORGE BUSH,
41ST U.S. PRESIDENT

27
Protection From Terrorism

Father, in the name of the Lord Jesus, I pray that You prevent the destructive forces of terrorism directed against our nation. Provide protection from evil attacks and stop the aggressors that attempt to bring destruction to our nation and people. May Your hand of protection keep us safe.

I stand against the spirit of fear that accompanies the cowardice acts of terrorism. Allow our fear to turn to trust in You. May knowledge of terrorist planned attacks be revealed to those who provide our national and international security. Help those in power to act swiftly to avert all danger, protecting American lives and property.

Provide strength, courage and wisdom to the protectors of this nation to administer their duties. Give wisdom and insight to our government and everyone involved in the elimination of terrorism. Provide instruction in the development of effective and efficient anti-terrorist strategies that will give us an advantage against our aggressors allowing the country to remain safe and secure.

I pray that the instigators of terrorism recognize the evil of their ways, and repent and denounce their cowardice acts of destruction against humanity. Without repentance, may they reap the consequences of their actions and may the fear of our retaliation be greater than their hatred of democracy.

Guide us in efforts to seek out and eradicate these merchants of death. Reveal the names of those responsible and in allegiance with terrorist organizations to our authorities. Enable the military to become swift, powerful and accurate in any action of retaliation.

Lord, help us to understand lifestyle changes that might be necessary to ensure our protection. Grant patience and tolerance to us in adapting to the safety precautions

and measures that we might experience.
Enable us to realize that the cost of
inconvenience is a small price to pay for the
safety of our families and of our nation.

Scripture References

Deuteronomy 29:29
Psalm 91:1-6
Daniel 11:25
Deuteronomy 31:6
Psalm 27:14

---

*The spirit of man is more important
than mere physical strength, and the
spiritual fiber of a nation than its wealth.*

—DWIGHT D. EISENHOWER,
34TH U.S. PRESIDENT

28
National Disaster

Father, in the name of the Lord Jesus, please direct our rescue workers in their labors, that survivors of disasters will be found in time. I pray that aid and support would arrive on every front.

May they come with the hope of not only finding the missing but also the means to feed the hungry, give drink to the thirsty and clothe the naked.

Help those in authority to make the right decisions. Show them ways to avoid and avert such tragedy in the future.

I pray that in the face of this tragedy, the gospel will be preached.

I pray that grieving families would be comforted.

Scripture References

Matthew 25:35,36
Isaiah 61:1-4
Mark 8:35

———

*We think it is incumbent upon this people
to humble themselves before God on
account of their sins...[And] also to
implore the Divine Blessing upon us,
that by the assistance of His grace, we may
be enabled to reform whatever is amiss
among us, that so God may be pleased
to continue to us the blessings we enjoy.*

—JOHN HANCOCK,
AMERICAN REVOLUTIONIST
AND THE FIRST SIGNER OF THE
DECLARATION OF INDEPENDENCE

Pray for Our Nation

29
In Time of War

Father, I come to You, in the name of our Lord Jesus, to lift up in prayer this present military action. Father, I pray that there might be a quick resolution to this action and that truth and righteousness would prevail.

May You guide, bless and protect all those engaged in this conflict. Heal the physical and spiritual wounds that may be inflicted.

Father, the gospel of the kingdom must be preached to this nation. I pray that what Satan has intended and devised to hinder the gospel You will turn to our good, that the gospel will go into this nation unimpeded.

Let all who hear Your Word turn to You for guidance, courage and hope.

Scripture References

1 Timothy 2:1-4
Matthew 24:14
Genesis 50:20

God presides over the destinies of nations.

—PATRICK HENRY,
AMERICAN REVOLUTIONIST

PART 4

Prayers for the Spiritual Growth of Our Nation

30
The Peace of Israel

Dear Father, I know that Israel is the apple of Your eye and that You hold her in the palm of Your hand. I know that soon Jesus will make His triumphal entry through the eastern gate at His return to the earth. Jerusalem will be the seat of government for all the earth.

I love Israel because You love Israel. I know that we have been blessed through her in the person of Jesus Christ.

Father, Jesus said that there would be unrest in Israel until He came again, because Israel will never know any real peace until the Prince of Peace returns. However, we are instructed to pray for the peace of Jerusalem so our prayers can help facilitate the events of His return.

In Jesus' mighty name, I pray for the peace of Jerusalem continually. I set myself as a watchman and will not rest until Jerusalem is a voice of praise in all the earth.

Scripture References

Matthew 24:6

Psalm 122:1

Isaiah 62:6,7

Genesis 12:3

Zechariah 2:8

Galatians 3:13,14,29

2 Peter 3:12 NIV

Direct my thought, words and work, wash away my sins in the immaculate Blood of the Lamb, and purge my heart by Thy Holy Spirit.... Daily frame me more and more into the likeness of Thy Son Jesus Christ.

—GEORGE WASHINGTON,
1ST U.S. PRESIDENT

31
National Revival

Father, in the name of Jesus, I pray for the great sleeping giant, the church, who even now has begun to shake herself from her sleep. I pray she would awake to righteousness and holiness in every denomination, in every body of believers, and slumber no longer.

I pray we would begin to unify under the blood-stained banner of the Cross and preach the gospel of the kingdom clearly and boldly in every highway and byway of our nation.

I pray that we will not only stand up and speak up but that we will begin to reap a great harvest in our nation, bringing multitudes to the saving knowledge of Jesus Christ.

May the revival of the saints be so all-encompassing that it affects the spiritual complexion of our entire nation and influences our politics, our economy, our media and our entire society.

Scripture References

Acts 3:19
Ephesians 3:14-21
Ephesians 1:15-23

Remember that God is our only sure trust.

—MARY WASHINGTON,
GEORGE WASHINGTON'S MOTHER

32
The Strengthening of the Family Unit

Father, it is apparent throughout Your Word that You instituted the family—father, mother and children. I realize, however, that a family unit can also consist of many other combinations, such as a husband and wife, a father and children, a mother and children or siblings.

I pray in the name of Jesus that the standard of a godly family would be restored to our nation.

May there be a resurgence in the public forum of the benefits of a godly family.

May it become apparent to those who form public opinion that family values as represented in Scripture are the path in which to lead our nation.

―――――

Scripture References

Genesis 1:28
Genesis 2:24
Leviticus 25:10
Numbers 36:6-8

―――――

Renewing our knowledge of and faith in God through Holy Scripture can strengthen us as a nation and a people.

―THE YEAR OF THE BIBLE
WAS DECLARED IN 1983 BY
A JOINT RESOLUTION OF
THE HOUSE AND SENATE

33
Church Leadership

Father, in the name of Jesus, I ask You to raise up persons of vision and purpose in the body of Christ, people of integrity who have the ability to unify and rally the body of Christ at large.

May they be godly examples to those whom they shepherd as they pray for Your guidance in every facet of their lives.

May they have the ability to make Your ways plain and clear, inspiring those who hear their words to seek a deep and abiding relationship with You, the Father of all.

Lord, give our church leaders a voice to speak to the conscience of our nation. May they not only influence the believer, but may they also influence those who have not yet come to know You as Lord and Savior. And may they use such words that would inspire and motivate our whole nation.

———

Scripture References

Proverbs 29:18
Luke 3:4-6 NIV
1 Timothy 3:1-13

———

While we give praise to God, the supreme disposer of all events, for His interposition on our behalf, let us guard against the dangerous error of trusting in, or boasting of, an arm of flesh....

If your case is just, if your principles are pure, and if your conduct is prudent, you need not fear the multitude of opposing hosts.

—JOHN WITHERSPOON,
A SIGNER OF THE DECLARATION
OF INDEPENDENCE

34
Deception

Dear Father, in the name of Jesus, I thank You that You have made me a child of the light. I thank You for Your holy written Word, which gives light to my path, and for the unction of the Holy Ghost, which leads me into all truth.

I pray that Your light would shine so brightly through the body of Christ that even the path our nation is to take will be illuminated by it.

May no deceiving person be successful in obtaining political office or able to influence governing decisions. And I pray that they will be exposed in their attempts to sway public opinion in their favor.

May truth and righteousness prevail in our nation from this day forward.

Scripture References

1 Thessalonians 5:1-6
John 16:13
Revelation 20:3
1 John 2:20
1 John 2:26,27 NAS
Psalm 119:105
John 17:17

There are a good many problems before the American people today, and before me as President, but I expect to find the solution to those problems just in the proportion that I am faithful in the study of the Word of God.

—WOODROW WILSON,
28TH U.S. PRESIDENT

Pray
for Our
Nation

35
Repentance

Dear Father, I come to You in the name of
Jesus Christ, my Advocate. I am so glad You
have not only made a way for me to be free
of sin, but you have also made a way for me
to stay that way.

Father, my heart condemns me because I
know I have sinned. [Name the sin.] I don't
have peace within me for I know I have
followed the desires of my heart and been
led into sin by allowing my feet to slip from
Your path. I ask You to forgive me and
cleanse me now.

I purpose in my heart not to do it again.
I realize, however, that I must constantly

seek Your help and direction to obtain that earnest desire.

I thank You that I am now clean and forgiven.

Scripture References

2 Chronicles 7:14
Isaiah 43:25,26
1 John 3:21,22
1 John 1:9,10;2:1,2
Psalm 17:5

Remember ever; and always, that your country was founded...by the stern old Puritans who made the deck of the Mayflower an altar of the living God, and whose first act on touching the soil of the new world was to offer on bended knees thanksgiving to Almighty God.

—HENRY WILSON,
18TH U.S. VICE PRESIDENT
UNDER ULYSSES S. GRANT

36
Prayer for the Salvation of Others

Father, I know that You are not willing that any should perish but desire that all should come to repentance. Therefore, I am praying for [unsaved person's name] and lifting him/her up to You today.

Satan, I command you in the name of the Lord Jesus Christ to take your hands off this person and to cease and desist in your maneuvers and activities against him/her.

Dear Father and Lord of the harvest, I claim [name] for Your kingdom and pray that You would send someone across his/her path to whom he/she can listen to and relate to.

Lord, I ask in the name of Jesus that You would give that laborer words that [name] cannot deny, so that the light of the glorious gospel would shine unto [name] and he/she will believe and be saved.

For all this I give You thanks in Jesus' wonderful name.

Scripture References

2 Peter 3:9

2 Corinthians 4:4

Ephesians 6:18,19

Matthew 18:18 NAS

Mathew 9:35-38

If we work on marble, it will perish; if on brass, time will efface it; if we rear up temples, they will crumble into dust; but if we work upon immortal minds and imbue them with principles, with the just fear of God and the love of our fellow men, we engrave on those tablets something that will brighten to all eternity.

—DANIEL WEBSTER,
AMERICAN POLITICIAN

37
Prayer for Personal Salvation

*Are you washed in the blood of the Lamb?
This is surely a question every person will
have to answer. What is your answer?*

*If your answer is no, then God is offering
an invitation to you today to receive the free
gift of salvation and become a member of
His ever-increasing family, a child of God.
Please pray this prayer now:*

Dear Father, I come to You in the name of
the Lord Jesus, knowing that as I call on His
name I shall be saved.

Your Word says that if I confess His name
with my mouth and believe in my heart that
You raised him from the dead, then I shall
be saved.

Dear Father, I truly believe that You raised Jesus Christ from the dead, and I say right now, "Jesus, You are my Lord." According to Your Word, I am saved now. I am Your very own child. Thank You, Father, for saving me and accepting me as Your very own.

Scripture References

John 6:37

Romans 10:9,10

Acts 4:12

Ephesians 1:6,7

Acts 2:21

Oh, Lord, Thou hast told us how to pray. Help us to shut the door, shutting out the world, and the enemy and any fear or doubt which spoils prayer. May there be no distance between our souls and Thee.

—JOHN WANAMAKER,
AMERICAN MERCHANT AND U.S.
POSTMASTER GENERAL FROM 1889-93

If you have prayed the prayer of salvation
for the first time while reading
this book, please write us
at the following address:

Harrison House
Tulsa, Oklahoma 74153

You may also visit the
Pray for Our Nation web-site at:
www.prayforournation.com

Additional copies of this book
are available from your local bookstore.

HARRISON HOUSE
Tulsa, Oklahoma 74153